The Schools We Want, The Schools We Deserve: American Education in Retrospect and Prospect

by
Denis P. Doyle

ISBN 0-87367-669-6

Copyright © 2000 by the Phi Delta Kappa Educational Foundation

Bloomington, Indiana

This fastback is sponsored by the
Suffolk County Chapter of Phi
Delta Kappa International, which made
a generous contribution toward
publication costs.

The chapter sponsors this fastback
to celebrate its 25th anniversary.

"A merely well-informed man is the most useless bore on God's earth. What we should aim at producing is men who possess both culture and expert knowledge in some special direction. Their expert knowledge will give them the ground to start from and their culture will lead them as deep as philosophy and as high as art."

— Alfred North Whitehead

"Perhaps the most valuable result of all education is the ability to make yourself do the thing you have to do, when it ought to be done, whether you like it or not; it is the first lesson that ought to be learned; and however early a man's training begins, it is probably the last lesson that he learns thoroughly."

— Thomas Henry Huxley

1

What have American schools been and what are they likely to become? Or perhaps more to the point — as suits a people at a pivotal point in their history — what have American schools been and what should they become? These are the narrow questions that this fastback attempts to answer. But in a great continental democracy, these questions are about more than education; they are about the future of the American experiment in self-government itself. The founders knew that democracy could flourish only with an educated citizenry. As Jefferson said in a letter to a friend in 1816, "If a nation expects to be ignorant and free, in a state of civilization, it expects what never was and never will be."

As past is prologue (proudly emblazoned over the entrance to the U.S. Archives), understanding where we have come from will help us to understand where we are going. The short history of American education is this: Our schools are a part of the larger culture in which they are embedded. Indeed, public schools are captives of their culture, followers not leaders, mirrors not telescopes. Education gathers up the past and hands it off to the future. It should come as no surprise to note that our modern school system — dating from the early 19th century — reflects the social order of which it is a part. One need not be a Marxist to know that schools replicate culture by transmitting it. Schools are conservative and schooling is a conservative institution. Slow to change, schools are traditional in the best sense of that term. As Chesterton reminds us, "tradition is the democracy of the dead."

Public schools are evolutionary, not revolutionary, institutions for good and sufficient reasons. Indeed, how could it be otherwise? Our regime is, after all, democratic capitalism. And there is no more finely calibrated system to give people what they want and desire with very little lag time. Our schools reflect this reality. Between the ballot box and the marketplace, preferences are communicated with stunning speed and accuracy. Although the coinage was Marxist, the practice is uniquely American: "Let a thousand flowers bloom." Where else but in the *Shopping Mall High School*, described so ably by Art Powell, Eleanor Farrar, and David Cohen.

True, the preferences the marketplace and the ballot box transmit may not be exalted or admirable; to the contrary, they often are vulgar and profane. But transmitted accurately and rapidly they are. Thus the fact that some schools spend more time and money on driver education or football or cheerleading than reading is a commentary on what we want and what we are. Truth be told, in America it may be that driving and football and cheerleading are more important than reading.

Attitudes of this kind come from within; they are not imposed on us by an unfriendly power. Unique in the world, our schools are overseen by elected (occasionally selected) school boards; they are examples of citizen democracy at work. Our culture is democratic (with a small d), egalitarian, and open. It is hard to escape the conclusion that we have both the schools we want and the schools we deserve.

But if schools reflect the values of the larger society generally, that is not to say that they are organizationally responsive institutions. Schools may be embedded in society, but as organizations they have their own compass. Where the internal life of the school is at variance with what its clients want, there may be sticking points. The principal feature in this picture is the bureaucratic arrangements that undergird school organization. Large organizations, particularly large monopolies and the bureaucracies that support them, develop lives of their own. They begin to march to their own drummer and minister first to their own needs and interests, only secondarily to the needs of their clients. Once ensconced, large, bureaucratic, and hierarchical organizations are slow to change, even in democratic societies.

But change they eventually will because change they must. Even though they do not exist in a conventional market, they can resist the entreaties and cajolery of their constituents only so long. If they foot-drag too much, they will lose their constituencies altogether, as is happening this very minute. At a conceptual level, this idea is more fully developed in Alfred O. Hirschman's elegant book, *Exit, Voice and Loyalty*. Hirschman makes the simple but powerful point that institutions that give their clients "voice" (and attend to it) gener-

9

ate loyalty; those that do not eventually lose their clients, the most discerning first, those they can least afford to lose. If this sounds like a description of modern public schooling, it is.

The closest parallel may be urban housing, where abandonment is a well-established and highly visible practice. In decaying housing markets the silent hulks of abandoned tenements stand in mute rebuke in city after city. So, too, school abandonment is a growing practice in the vast majority of the nation's larger cities, a sign of institutional and intellectual decay. Those that can leave do; those that cannot leave stay because they must.

2

It is true that on occasion schools give the impression of being at the forefront of social debate and concern — civil rights issues, prayer, condom distribution, creationism, OBE, vouchers — but these issues simply reemphasize the fact that schools follow, not lead. As Oliver Wendell Holmes dryly observed, the little boy who rushes to the head of the circus parade may be marching in front, but he is not leading. Nonetheless, it is true that schools are a major arena in which social issues materialize. After all, they are second only to health in the amount of GDP they consume — $360 billion in 1998-99 for elementary and secondary education alone — and with 45 million students, they directly involve 20% of the nation's population.

Schools, if not leaders, are nonetheless stages on which national and regional dramas play out. The most enduring example of national cultural and political drama in which schools have figured prominently has been civil rights. In the 19th century the issue was religion; in the 20th, race. Indeed, religion and public schools are an old story in America. The first schools for the public in the New World appeared in the 17th century in the

Massachusetts Bay Colony. Initiated under the terms of the Old Deluder Satan Act in 1645, their purpose was to see that literacy was diffused among the population at large. Being able to read and know their Bible, citizens could escape Satan's temptations.

The modern public school came into being more than a century later under the sponsorship of Governor DeWitt Clinton in the early 19th century. As a philanthropist, business leader, inventor, and governor, Clinton was concerned that, though numerous, private schools — almost exclusively religious — could not meet society's need for broadly based education. To remedy this deficit, he created the Free School Society, recognizing that denominational schools concentrated on their own congregants. Early on, Clinton realized that private subscriptions were inadequate and sought public funds, which not only forced a name change — it soon became the Public School Society — but placed control in the hands of public officials.

Within a generation, public schools became relentlessly Protestant, with obligatory prayer and Bible reading limited to the King James (or Protestant) Bible. The Catholic Bible — the Douay — would not do. Waves of Catholic immigration fueled increasingly intense anti-Catholic sentiment among a largely Protestant population, and by 1847 Catholic schools (infelicitously known as Irish schools) had been systematically disenfranchised by state legislatures. They no longer received public funds. Catholics (against whom the campaign was mounted) faced a Hobson's choice: If they remained in government schools, they could read any prayer they liked so long as it was Protestant. (So, too, could other non-Protestants.) The disenfranchisement of Catholic public schools led to the creation, halfway through the century, under the sponsorship of Bishop Hughes of New York, of the modern Catholic school system.

Public schools were to remain steadfastly Protestant until 1962, when the U.S. Supreme Court struck down prayer in public schools altogether. (Perhaps not altogether. As Al Shanker wryly noted, any time a math test is given at least some of the students are praying in school.)

So intense was anti-Catholic sentiment that James G. Blaine has been immortalized for his namesake amendment. A friend of President Grant, he tried repeatedly to enact a Blaine amendment to the U.S. Constitution that had one purpose only: to forbid aid to Catholic schools. There were several important aspects to his quixotic quest. It revealed, of course, the depth of anti-Catholic sentiment in the young nation and it also revealed the fact that it was politically correct to talk about it in public. Even more important, however, was the fact that it highlighted the constitutionality of aid to religious schools unless there was an amendment forbidding it. Not until 1947 did the U.S. Supreme Court develop a doctrine of separation of church and state that forbade transfer payments for religiously oriented education.

While a Blaine amendment was not enacted at the federal level, Blaine amendments were enacted in more than 30 states, where they remain in effect to this day. Thus the threshold test for aid to religious schools is substantially higher in many states than at the federal level.

Not surprisingly, the question of support for Catholic schools was one of the major reasons the federal government did not become involved in funding elementary and secondary education until two-thirds of the way through the 20th century. To only slightly exaggerate, Catholics were afraid that a federal program would ignore them, Protestants were afraid a federal program would not. So, too, Northerners thought federal aid would exclude blacks, Southerners thought such a program would include them. And everyone, it seems, North and South, East and West, feared a loss of local control. The predictable result was stalemate.

Not until President Johnson did the Congress enact federal aid for elementary and secondary schools — at a price. Big-city Democrats extracted a promise from Johnson: aid for Catholic schools. Enter Title I, the first major program of federal aid to American school children across the board. It included public and nonpublic schools. This pattern was to reappear in the Carter years. (Johnson's task was made easier by the *Brown* decision a decade earlier; if, as a practical matter, invidious racial segregation had not ended, at least public policy was clear. There was no longer a policy debate about racial justice at the federal level.)

Running for president, Mr. Carter had promised to create a Department of Education with its own secretary; he, too, failed to reckon with big-city Democrats and their Catholic constituents. They delivered their votes for the department only after extracting a promise *in writing* that Mr. Carter would create the position of non-statutory assistant secretary for nonpublic education. To complete the cycle, Mr. Reagan, an ardent supporter of private education, eliminated the position as a bit of cost-cutting symbolism. It was one of the few federal jobs he could cut by executive order.

By way of contrast, in the 20th century the public school civil rights issue was race, not religion; and it was decided on behalf of the plaintiffs, reversing a century and one half of "separate but equal," a legal doctrine so dubious that to this day it is hard to fathom. *Brown* v. *Board of Education* was the signal judicial event of the 20th century.

But even so noble a cause as *Brown* has had its uncertainties and disappointments. While the cause of racial justice embodied by *Brown* was unambiguous, school busing for racial balance was hardly an unambiguous success. It is not clear, for example — with the virtue of hindsight — that the money and time poured into the cause might not have been invested more fruitfully in other ways. Better schools for low-achieving youngsters, for example. Being bused because of your race from one ordinary school to another is a Pyrrhic victory, and being bused from a bad school to another bad school is no victory at all.

Indeed, it is sobering from this vantage point to remember the injury for which the Brown family sought redress. The Brown's child was being bused — involuntarily — from her neighborhood to a school across town. A black child, she was bused to a black school. The remedy the Brown family sought — and won — was the right to walk to her neighborhood school. By such a straightforward expedient was invidious racial segregation in the schools summarily struck down.

3

But if there is many a slip twixt cup and lip in the world of schooling, there is more that reflects continuity than discontinuity, more that reflects similarity than dissimilarity.

Schooling, it has been noted before, is one of the few social activities we engage in that Socrates would presumably recognize were he to return from the grave. Slow, labor intensive, formal education is a process in which the old impart their knowledge to the young (even the Socratic method, built on questions rather than answers, fits this description). To be sure, changes have occurred; Guttenberg's development of printing makes mass education possible (though it fell to Jan Comenius, the Great Didactic, to invent the textbook). But possibility is not certainty, just as necessary conditions are not sufficient conditions.

After the textbook came mass-produced, inexpensive workbooks (replacing the hornbook) and mass-produced lead pencils, so inexpensive that students could possess their own. Not only could students take notes in class, they also could do homework, first by candlelight, then by electric light.

Electrification, of course, permitted the genuine technological innovations of the 20th century to appear: the centrally synchronized school clock and bell, then the teacher's time clock (to punch in, thanks to Frederick Taylor and his scientific management minions). Then there appeared the most invasive technology, the public address system, making the modern school even more like the modern factory (or prison, if you like). Finally, as Ralph Tyler irreverently noted, one instructional technology finally emerged (because it was simple enough for teachers to use): the overhead projector.

It is important to note that these technologies, without exception, are "more of the same" technologies, not transforming technologies. "More of the same" technologies may do old things faster or better or cheaper, but they are fundamentally similar in purpose and function. By way of illustration, the horseless carriage was an extension of existing technology; when it became the automobile, a quantitative transformation had occurred. Not surprisingly, we still measure mechanical capacity with the term *horsepower*. Old ideas die hard.

By way of contrast, consider medicine. It, too, was unchanged from the time of Socrates (or Hippocrates, if you prefer) till the mid-19th century. But unlike education, *transforming* medical technologies appeared that changed the way in which medicine was understood and practiced. (At the end of the 19th century, Harvard President Elliott solemnly declared that medicine was science, not art, permitting Harvard to award the degree, Doctor of Medicine. Even at the end of the 20th century, no such claim can be advanced for education.)

The great transforming medical technologies were three (with numerous variations on a theme): antisepsis, anesthesia, and antibiotics. Each provided new and powerful insights into treatment and care. Until they appeared, medicine was an arcane art, practiced in privacy if not secrecy. Indeed, some medical breakthroughs — obstetrical forceps, for example — were kept secret for decades by jealous inventors determined to protect their monopoly position.

Antisepsis, based on the germ theory of disease, arose from the work of Pasteur and Lister. Their remarkable insight was that pathogens cause illness, some of which may be cured by appropriate treatment and, *mirabile dictu*, some of which may actually be prevented by appropriate prevention protocols, ranging from such homespun activities as pure water or the more arcane practices of vaccination (inspired by smallpox-free milkmaids).

As amazing as germ theory was, in some respects anesthesia was more remarkable because its properties are even more nearly magical: anesthesia permits a physician to enter the body without causing pain or death. It rolls the tape backwards, as it were, permitting the physician to undo what was made wrong by trauma, disease process, or heredity. And as important as anesthesia is in its own right, it ushered in an extraordinarily powerful downstream activity that is even more important: the operating *theater*. The operating theater is precisely what its name says it is. The operating theater is where the senior surgeon shows her stuff. It is the place where physicians in training (and other health professionals) *come to learn*. It is the ultimate teaching device, made possible by anesthesia. It is the place where senior professionals hone their skills and where the baton of knowledge is passed.

Then there are antibiotics, the stuff of life itself (or, to be precise, anti-life). It is well known from both macro- and micro-parasitism that one form of life can destroy another. Until antibiotics, however, the street was one way, the wrong way. With antibiotics, medicine was transformed. The microbial life that would injure or even kill its host can itself be destroyed. The story of the discovery of penicillin is so widely known that it would hardly bear retelling except for its relevance to medicine's companion discipline, education. Alexander Fleming (soon to be Sir Alexander, thanks to his discovery) was pottering about in his laboratory. Attempting to clean petri dishes, he could not get rid of a pesky mold. It kept coming back for more. It was irrepressible. To everyone but Fleming, it was a nuisance. It fell to Fleming to understand that the "mold that would not die" was an asset, not a liability. It was from this mold that he produced penicillin, the first and most famous of the antibiotics.

4

As we examine the future of education we shall return to medicine as metaphor. At this point, suffice it to say that as medicine was becoming more scientific, in important respects education was becoming less scientific. To be sure, there emerged, among educators, a passionate commitment to "scientific management," but in this context the term obscures as much as it reveals. Adopting it as a mantra symbolized a scientific wrong turn. Why? Truth be told, scientific management was more management than science. To be sure, it was effective; it was thorough and systematic; it was careful and calibrated; it was ingenious and became widespread. As Peter Drucker notes, Frederick Taylor, its founder, was a genius of sorts. But it is also the case that scientific management was first a strategy to improve industrial production and only later adapted to public administration. And in a school setting it veered from its original trajectory, which was to improve output. Inspired in a factory setting, it was hostile to professionalism because its guiding purpose — and most ringing success — was to institutionalize the suspension of judgment. Scientific management spared workers — teachers in the schools — the burden of thinking and decision making. And, irony of ironies, it is only in schools that scientific management survives today.

Scientific management, designed to rationalize workflow, inhibits good teachers; it does not liberate them. It eliminates human error by simplifying work. At the same time it limits human creativity. Its greatest power was to *deskill* the workforce or, more charitably, to permit employers to use an unskilled workforce by making work so straightforward that anyone could do it. That, of course, was the triumph of the assembly line. A strong back, deft hands, a willing attitude: that was all that was required. In a school setting, scientific management meant "teacher-proofing" the classroom. It meant organizing the work of teachers in such a way that they could not get it wrong. It was the precise opposite of professionalism, just as the assembly line was the precise opposite of skilled craftsmanship.

That is why, to this day, the creative teacher is so often a "canny outlaw," a person who bends the rules to do the job in a way that is both more interesting and more satisfying. The imaginative and inventive teacher knows that once her door is closed, she can abandon the required lesson plan and do what she thinks is best. She does not ask, she acts. As Sy Fliegel is fond of saying, it is "easier to ask for forgiveness than seek permission."

It is worth remembering that "teacher-proofing" the classroom was not part of a plot to reduce the competence of teachers or downgrade the profession. Rather, it reflected the realities of the day. It was even well-intentioned. A booming industrial economy, massive migration (both internal and from across the sea), rapid urbanization, and an increasingly complex social order made mass education a virtual necessity. Hard on the heels of the Civil War, enormous numbers of children (and their families) had to be socialized to the new social and economic order that was materializing. There were simply not enough competent teachers.

The size and scale of the changes that were under way were so vast that they are hard to comprehend, even with our long view. The agricultural revolution, which went hand in hand with the industrial revolution, is illustrative. At the beginning of the 19th century, 95% of the nation lived on the land. Most Americans were self-sufficient, and whatever surplus they produced fed and clothed the remainder. By the end of the 19th century the number had fallen to 50%; by the end of the 20th the number has fallen to 2.5% and continues to fall. Even more striking, that 2.5% feeds not just America but much of the world; and the biggest agricultural problem of the past half-century has been managing overabundance, not scarcity.

Mass production's corollary is, of course, mass education. The appearance of the public school — on a large scale — and the explosive growth of enrollment required a corresponding explosion in the growth of school workers. Just as Henry Ford needed workers for his assembly lines, the schools needed workers for theirs. It comes as no surprise to learn that they were not all cast in Albert Einstein's mold. Nor should it come as a surprise that they were not cast in the mold of the skilled craftsman or professional. It was, after all, mass education, and they were cast in the mold of the industrial worker.

As schooling grew in size, scope, and scale, a significant bridge had to be crossed. What was schooling's purpose in an industrializing democracy? Was it to provide a liberal education, as elites had been educated historically? The Committee of Ten thought so. Created in 1892, it comprised 100 distinguished Americans (including Princeton President Woodrow Wilson). The Committee of Ten was committed to education reform (much as the *Nation at Risk* panel was more than a century later) modeled on British practice. They, too, issued a clarion call for high academic standards. It not only fell on deaf ears, within a generation the NEA issued a counter-manifesto: the *14 Cardinal Principles*. A ringing endorsement of life-adjustment education, it called for "education of the whole child." John Dewey had also called for the education of the whole child, but he did not mean to abandon academics. The authors of the *14 Cardinal Principles* did, and they were successful; no longer would high academic standards be the core enterprise of schooling. The systematic study of the liberal arts, except for the college bound, was not to be a part of public education

The idea was not without foundation. Romanticism fueled the movement. As it was good enough for poets, it was good enough for the new pedagogy. E.D. Hirsch brilliantly tells the story in *The Schools We Need and Why We Don't Have Them*, and I will not retell it here. But one point is germane; as Richard Hofstadter observes in his timeless classic, *Anti-Intellectualism in American Life*, schools did not then and do not now escape the American disdain for the examined life.

That we are pragmatic is not all bad; to be sure, pragmatism is useful. (Pragmatism and transcendentalism are America's twin contributions to philosophical thought, an unlikely pair if ever there was one.) But the fact remains: We are a relentlessly practical people; and in practical matters, pragmatism has stood us in good stead. It is no accident that the assembly line is an American invention, and it would be hard to overestimate its importance as a way to produce wealth on an unparalleled scale. And not just for the owner of capital. Henry Ford saw to it that his assembly line workers could afford to buy their own products, an idea so widely accepted today that it is hard to understand how revolutionary it was less than a century ago. (It is equaled, no doubt, by Peter Drucker's extraordinary insight that today — not quite as Marx had imagined — workers own the means of production. Pension fund socialism, he calls it.)

We have, then, a school system well designed to produce workers for an industrialized economy. Academic excellence, mastery of the liberal arts, was for the small proportion of students who would go on to college or university. Top-end graduates would become managers, engineers, ministers, designers, teachers, architects, lawyers, doctors, policy analysts, and overseers: in Aldous Huxley's *Brave New World* they are the Alphas. The less talented would go on to two-year colleges, the military, vocational and technical training, or apprenticeships to take their place as technicians in the goods-producing economy. The least talented fill the ranks of semi-skilled and unskilled labor.

However well or poorly these patterns of preparation worked for most of the century, they are almost wholly out of synch with the knowledge-based, post-industrial economy of today. The issue is cast in high relief at both ends of the spectrum. At the low-skill end, there are few slots for the unskilled, and the few slots that exist pay less than ever before. Indeed, as John Bishop's work points out, not only are the incomes of those with a high school diploma or less falling relatively, they are falling absolutely. The lack of higher education (except for entertainers and sports stars) condemns most people to lives of penury. Indeed, the least skilled among us find that, worse than being condemned to a life of menial work, they may be condemned to a life of no work. Horatio Alger is dead. Luck and pluck are still desirable, but they are no longer sufficient (if ever they were).

The truth is this: Education pays and it pays handsomely. Or as Harvard President Derek Bok says, "if you think education is expensive, try ignorance." But what kind of elementary and secondary education pays? Vocational? Technical? General? Academic? What should youngsters know and be able to do to earn a diploma? The answer is not so hard to find as might be imagined. Look to two sources: world-class schools and the traits that employers say they look for in new employees and consider for promotion.

5

Knowing labor markets, the first hurdle an employer must pass over is whether to "make it or buy it." By this they mean, Can they hire a person already trained or must they do the training themselves? They look first for whatever special skills are associated with the jobs that need to be done — engineering, law, turret lathe operator, x-ray technician, computer programmer, or whatever. If they are unable to find suitably trained people, they then face another choice unique to the global economy: train or outsource (frequently going offshore).

The advent of the telecommunications revolution, together with an international regime of relatively free trade, means that today's firm is not restricted to domestic labor markets. As Peter Drucker notes, one of the triumphs of the industrial revolution was "moving workers to their work." The corresponding triumph of the postindustrial revolution is "moving work to workers." This means more than occasional telecommuting within a traditional domestic labor market. It means global telecommuting in both goods and services markets. Computer programmers, for example, can program as readily in Bombay as they can in Silicon Valley or Silicon Glen (Scotland) without the inconvenience and expense of moving. And without the inconvenience and expense — to the employer — of American salaries and fringe benefits. The example is not hypothetical. It is going on today, and the process will only accelerate.

It is important to note that Indian or Scottish computer programmers are in demand not just because they "cost" less than domestic programmers — though that is attractive to employers — but because they are available and they are good. In fact, they are better than good; they are outstanding. Indian mathematics education is of the highest quality and Indian traditions of mathematical accomplishment are of long standing. So, too, Scotland. It is no surprise that they stand ready to enter the international global economy. The historic surprise is that the economy is coming to them. American workers are entering a genuinely global economy.

No matter how employers handle the issue of specific skills — make it, buy it, go offshore — they express a strong preference for a set of collateral attributes: communication skills, the capacity to solve problems, the ability to work with different people in different settings, the capacity to continue learning on the job, the ability to work in teams, honesty, punctuality, reliability. Indeed, survey after survey reveals that most employers assert that, all things being equal, these attributes are more important than specific job skills. In *Investing in Our Children: Business and the Schools*, a 1985 policy statement of the Committee for Economic Development for which I was project director and co-author, we used the term *invisible curriculum* to both demarcate and high-light these capacities. As important as they are, how they are acquired is significant. Quaker schools have a term of art to describe it: values are "caught, not taught." They are in the air. They are imparted by example, study, and practice.

Students who are permitted to wear hats in class, turn in assignments late (or not at all), and be disrespectful of teachers and fellow students are being sent a strong message — anything goes. That it is not true makes it all the more pernicious. Sending this message does no one a favor, not the student, not the school, not the larger society. It works a cruel hoax on everyone in the system.

By way of contrast, a school that imparts lessons about intellectual rigor also imparts lessons about be-havior, demeanor, and deportment that will stand the student in good stead for as long as he or she lives. Care-lessness, sloth, and disrespect do not produce thought-fully wrought essays or successful lab work; nor do they produce subject matter mastery. Of whom much is expected much will be produced. Most important, ex-pecting much of students is a sign of respect, and students know it. Expecting little or, worse yet, nothing is an expression of contempt.

What is analytically clear is that employers look for peo-ple who are "liberally educated" in the old and honorable sense of that term. (Rare are the employers who use the term, "liberally educated," but that is what they mean.) To be liberally educated in the ancient world meant to possess an education suited for a free man. *Liberalis*. It was both a sign of freedom and it was liberating.

A liberal education — mastery of the arts and sciences, history and philosophy, rhetoric and declamation — frees the mind and frees the man or woman. But is it not still the case that vocational education is the key to economic success? Three points are germane.

First is the view of John Henry Cardinal Newman, who, writing his magnum opus, *The Uses of the University*, in the mid-19th century, argued that a liberal education was sufficient unto itself. It had no vocational purpose. Unlike vocational education that had a discrete purpose, a liberal education's only purpose was to improve the mind. That is an elegant formulation with an obvious debt to Classical Greece, but not one suited to move a pragmatic people.

David T. Kearns, then CEO of Xerox, captured the second piece of the puzzle when he said, "business will train if the schools educate." That is, the foundation on which vocational preparation rests is a liberal education. Training is not the same as education; and however valuable training is, it cannot and should not be confused with education. Education is, at one level, a profoundly moral undertaking. It does not communicate information at random. The organized body of information that a liberal arts education imparts is designed to make the student a better man or woman, a person capable of making discerning judgments about applying technical and vocational knowledge.

Finally, I would argue that today the only truly vocational education is a liberal education. Why? Because as George Santayana would have it, a liberal education provides the "furniture of the mind." It is the education that prepares people to think, to reason, to communicate, to create. It also imparts those attributes that we have come to think of as the invisible curriculum that employers prize. A liberal education confers precisely what the modern economy rewards most highly, habits of mind and judgment that make it possible to use information and technology wisely and well. A liberally educated person can secure vocational education readily.

Where should a liberal education begin? It should begin in the early grades and reach full flower in high school. It may continue in college — indeed, it should — but that should not be its only home.

Are there examples of liberal arts high schools? There are. In a democracy such as ours, the world-class high school is, by definition, the school that enrolled the First Child, Ms. Clinton. (It also enrolled the Gores' son.) The First and Second Families, well informed and well connected, could enroll their children in any school they chose, day or boarding, public or private. Why did they choose Sidwell Friends, a Quaker day school? Because of what it teaches and how it teaches. Because of its intellectual values. What are its salient characteristics? Sidwell offers a liberal education and high academic standards in an ethical setting. Racially and socioeconomically integrated, Sidwell is a school in the Quaker tradition. Of its students and faculty it expects honesty, self-respect, and respect for others, just as it expects high levels of academic accomplishment. Indeed, the two are reciprocals. To achieve at high levels, students must be honest, hard working, tolerant, open minded, responsible, and respectful.

6

If world-class schools are few and far between (and hard to get into) what of those schools that remain? As I have suggested, they have two major deficiencies. One is a simple reflection of the larger society: a relentless anti-intellectualism. The other reflects bureaucracy everywhere: organizational rigidity. What is to be done in the face of these twin threats to excellence? The stock answers are several: Conservatives decry unionization, liberals despair over lack of money. Conservatives argue that the stranglehold of the bureaucracy can be broken only by privatization and vouchers. Many liberals and most conservatives support higher academic standards but do not agree as to who should set them; in particular, liberals distrust local control and conservatives support it, and liberals trust the national government in education matters while conservatives do not. In the case of national standards, Checker Finn has wryly observed that they will not come to pass because liberals distrust anything with the word "standards" in it, conservatives distrust anything with the word "national" in it.

There is one issue, one policy debate, that captures these differences. It is a freighted word, *vouchers*. To opponents it conjures up images of the destruction of the public schools, to supporters it promises a welcome breath of freedom in an otherwise oppressive regime. I am convinced that neither side is correct; if enacted, vouchers will not spell the end of public education, neither will they be a panacea.

Public education is simply too big, too robust, and too important to be swept aside by vouchers. Only if public schools lose their moorings altogether and fail utterly to meet their obligations to their students will they be at risk — as they are in many of our great cities today; that is a cautionary tale if ever there was one. But public schools in small towns and villages, in medium-size cities and suburbs, in the rural hinterland retain their vitality and enjoy substantial public support. True, they are institutions in transition (which may make them look as if they are in trouble) but they are not troubled institutions. As a professional interested in education I have visited dozens of schools over the past five years — East and West, North and South, urban, suburban, and rural — and they are vibrant, energetic institutions, staffed by talented men and women. Interestingly, many of the most exciting schools I visit are open-enrollment institutions, places where children have decided to go and teachers decided to teach. They are "communities of scholarship," precisely what distinguishes good from ordinary schools.

Vouchers, then, will make a small but significant difference on the margins. But the big issue is not vouchers. Vouchers are still the stuff of ideology; they are not yet the stuff of pragmatism. Only if the middle class sees vouchers as a pragmatic solution will they come to pass, for the middle class in a democracy cannot be denied. And if the middle class is moved to support vouchers, it will be because the American middle class has lost faith in public schooling altogether. As we have seen, that has come very close to happening in our great cities. But only the public schools themselves can induce such an outcome — to do so they would have to forfeit an enormous reservoir of good will. But that is what it would take, a failure of supply, not an excess of demand.

Because schools follow the clues offered by the larger culture, the place to look for signs of change is to briefly examine major domestic and global issues. Or as Daniel Yergin says in his book of the same title, look at the "commanding heights." Of those that have a bearing on education, there are four: standards, choice, technology, and knowledge-based decision making. I return to them to close the essay. But there is one more piece of the record that has a bearing on the future of American schools.

I performed an impromptu analysis of my own Chicago high school transcript: about 3,200 hours of academic instruction in four years. In addition to quantity was quality: the *Iliad*, the *Odyssey*, the *Aneid*, the *Song of Roland*, *Romeo and Juliet*, *Julius Caesar*, *Hamlet*. True, the Chicago public school authorities thought that Shakespeare in the original was too racy for tender minds, which had the unintended consequence of turning some of us into Shakespeare scholars. Nothing like searching for expurgated passages to turn a teenager into a careful reader. With good teaching leading the way, content, quality, and contact hours make a difference.

By the time William Bennett was Secretary of Education, Chicago's glory years (the late 1950s) were long gone. His comment that Chicago's public schools were the worst in the nation was a stinging rebuke not just to alumni, but to people everywhere who cared about education excellence. It may not have been literally true, but it was a symbol of urban decay that we could neither deny nor evade. Our great city schools had at one time set the pace. No longer.

But the "city of big shoulders" is reclaiming its legacy. Chicago is pulling back from the brink precisely because Mayor Daley, School Board Chair Gery Chico, and Superintendent Paul Vallas are committed to a performance-driven school system.

They support as wide a variety of delivery mechanisms as can be imagined so long as the schools deliver. Their message is a simple one: standards, standards, standards. The old rhetoric about public versus private is disappearing. Micromanagement is disappearing.

Citizen participation is increasing. Test scores are climbing. Teen pregnancy is dropping. Why? Chicago is entering a post-ideological era. Vallas asks, "What works?"

For example, Vallas is interested in Catholic schools not for ideological or religious reasons but because they keep their academic promises, particularly for poor and minority youngsters. As a public school CEO, Vallas looks to the competition for insights into how to improve his own schools. He is not afraid of competition, he welcomes it. His relationship with private schools makes the point. He meets regularly with the head of the diocesan schools to find out what they are doing that works.

One thing that works is clearly defined and delineated graduation standards. He has borrowed Catholic high school graduation standards to create public high school graduation standards. He knows — and is not afraid of knowing — that imitation is the sincerest form of flattery. And he knows his clientele — the people of Chicago. Many of them — one-third — prefer parochial schools to public schools, yet the double financial burden of taxes and tuition are crushingly heavy. About vouchers, tax credits, and other schemes to provide support for nonpublic schools, Vallas is agnostic. He neither supports nor opposes such ideas. He leaves those issues to the political process. He will live with whatever the public supports. As he sees it, his job is to do the best he can with what he has. And one of the things he "has" is the authority to issue charters. Vallas, in a bold move, has invited Catholic schools to apply for "charters."

8

If organizational rigidity is the problem and institutional flexibility is the answer, how can it be accomplished on a large scale? It is not simply a matter of throwing away the keys, burning the red tape, and turning schools lose. School districts and the public officials responsible for them still must exercise fiduciary responsibility for their charges. Among other things, they are legally liable for whatever happens; more to the point, they are morally liable for what happens. To leave a child — or worse yet, groups of children — uneducated in the 21st century is a form of moral hazard.

But if, as I have suggested, it also is the case that schools follow, not lead, what are the major trends in the larger society that set the die for schools as the next century begins? As I have already noted, four elements of the larger cultural context will change schooling irrevocably: standards, knowledge-based decision making, choice, and technology.

Standards are the key to school reform. They are the necessary, if not sufficient, first step. But they do not exist in a vacuum. Standards must be set, they must be met, and there must be consequences for meeting them — rewards — and penalties for failing to meet them.

Standards describe what candidates must know and be able to do to earn a diploma. Some observers parse standards into two parts: content standards are what students should know, performance standards are how well they know them. No matter how the ideas are presented, one overwhelming fact stands out: a standards-based education leads ineluctably to a performance-driven system. If what you know is important — as distinct from how long you have been in school — the old paradigm evaporates. No longer are schools measured by inputs — what goes into them. In the modern era they will be measured by outputs — what they produce.

This is not to say that inputs are not important. To the contrary, their relationship to outputs — and to use the dreadful term of computer art, throughput — must be rationalized. What schools do with what they get determines what the output will be. Instructional programs make a difference, and how and in what way they make a difference must be fully understood for schools to be successful. As *Prisoners of Time* observed, for 150 years time has been fixed and academic performance variable. In the school of the future, time will be the variable, high levels of academic performance fixed.

The triptych of standards, assessments, and consequences is hardly unique to schools. It is evident in each and every successful enterprise, private or public, profit or nonprofit, large or small. Indeed, not long ago it was assumed that schools exhibited a commitment to this format. The curriculum embodied standards, teacher grades were the assessment, and consequences were

9

Knowledge-based decision making is an idea so obvious and commonsensical it is hard to imagine that it is not the norm. Is there any other way to make decisions? Unhappily, the answer is "yes." The most obvious examples are political and personal, two styles that are often conflated. Log rolling and patronage are among the most egregious examples. But there is a less widely discussed example of decision making that is not knowledge-based that has a bearing on the school of the future, and that is decision making by intuition. So common is this among great leaders that it is almost a sign of greatness. Examples come readily to mind, from Winston Churchill to Lincoln, from Alexander to FDR. It also is the case that intuition plays a major role in hard disciplines. Jeremy Bernstein, Einstein's biographer, reports that Einstein's great insights were first the product of mathematical intuition, only later "proved" mathematically. Indeed, some of Einstein's work exceeded his own mathematical capacities and it fell to a later generation of physicists to demonstrate that he was correct.

Standards describe what candidates must know and be able to do to earn a diploma. Some observers parse standards into two parts: content standards are what students should know, performance standards are how well they know them. No matter how the ideas are presented, one overwhelming fact stands out: a standards-based education leads ineluctably to a performance-driven system. If what you know is important — as distinct from how long you have been in school — the old paradigm evaporates. No longer are schools measured by inputs — what goes into them. In the modern era they will be measured by outputs — what they produce.

This is not to say that inputs are not important. To the contrary, their relationship to outputs — and to use the dreadful term of computer art, throughput — must be rationalized. What schools do with what they get determines what the output will be. Instructional programs make a difference, and how and in what way they make a difference must be fully understood for schools to be successful. As *Prisoners of Time* observed, for 150 years time has been fixed and academic performance variable. In the school of the future, time will be the variable, high levels of academic performance fixed.

The triptych of standards, assessments, and consequences is hardly unique to schools. It is evident in each and every successful enterprise, private or public, profit or nonprofit, large or small. Indeed, not long ago it was assumed that schools exhibited a commitment to this format. The curriculum embodied standards, teacher grades were the assessment, and consequences were manifold — high grades meant accolades and success, low grades (or worse yet, failing grades) meant disappointment and failure. To this day many Americans think that our schools still work this way, as indeed the best ones do. Boston Latin, Sidwell Friends, Brooklyn Tech, St. Paul's, Bronx Science are free-standing institutions that have established their own high standards. They meet them because they want to, and the consequences are there for all to see.

This deceptively simple formulation is relatively easy to achieve in small institutions with high degrees of social consensus. Each of the schools listed above is selective, each is demanding, each knows what it is doing and why. And the students in them know what is expected of them and why what is expected of them makes sense.

It also is relatively easy to achieve in large systems with very high degrees of social consensus: Singapore, Korea, Japan, French *Lycées*, German *Gymnasia*, Italian *Lyceos*. In these settings, standards are high, performance is excellent, and consequences are real. A common syllabus is used in every school in the system, as is a common curriculum. Not surprisingly, national exit examinations are required to earn a degree. So uniform is the French system, we are told, that the French Minister of Education can tell you what page in which book any child in France is on at any given hour and day. A more realistic but no less important illustration is not apocryphal: French schools do not issue transcripts of record; instead, the *baccalaureate* is awarded in three degrees: *bien*, *assez bien*, and *tres bien*. All employ-

40

ers in France know precisely what these distinctions mean. They are valid, useful, and accurate. And they have consequences for students.

In large, diverse American systems, however, with children from widely different backgrounds and teachers with widely different patterns of preparation, centrifugal force — rather than social consensus — is the prime characteristic. Accountability is the rage in America precisely because social consensus about what schools should be doing is absent. Or more properly, the social consensus that exists is so fluid that it is almost impossible to measure.

•

9

Knowledge-based decision making is an idea so obvious and commonsensical it is hard to imagine that it is not the norm. Is there any other way to make decisions? Unhappily, the answer is "yes." The most obvious examples are political and personal, two styles that are often conflated. Log rolling and patronage are among the most egregious examples. But there is a less widely discussed example of decision making that is not knowledge-based that has a bearing on the school of the future, and that is decision making by intuition. So common is this among great leaders that it is almost a sign of greatness. Examples come readily to mind, from Winston Churchill to Lincoln, from Alexander to FDR. It also is the case that intuition plays a major role in hard disciplines. Jeremy Bernstein, Einstein's biographer, reports that Einstein's great insights were first the product of mathematical intuition, only later "proved" mathematically. Indeed, some of Einstein's work exceeded his own mathematical capacities and it fell to a later generation of physicists to demonstrate that he was correct.

There is nothing wrong with these approaches so far as the individual examples are concerned. Would that we all had the insights of Churchill or Einstein. But that is precisely the problem. Brilliant intuition may lead to brilliant insights, but ordinary intuition does not. More to the point, an enterprise such as mass education cannot rely on the hope that visionary leaders will head every school. In one respect the old scientific management movement was right: Decision making should be orderly, it should be informed by facts, it should be supported by rigorous analysis, and it should be subject to constant re-analysis and reinterpretation.

I noted earlier that I would return to my medical metaphor; it is especially appropriate here. We have seen medicine's debt to science; indeed, to this day the notion of medicine man means a traditional or nonscientific practitioner. This serves to remind us that medicine is by no means all science, even in the modern era — it is still in some measure art. In particular, the art of the healer is made manifest in what we call "bedside manner," the capacity of the physician to empathize with the patient as a means to reassure, diagnose, and treat. To the trained physician, much decision making can be attributed to informed intuition, particularly when there is no definitive test or diagnostic protocol. Particularly under the pressure of relentless deadlines, someone must decide in conditions of uncertainty and ambiguity. This is particularly important in light of the widely accepted experience shared by most physicians: The vast majority of presenting cases — patients who show up at the doctor's office with symptoms — spontaneously resolve. That is, they are neither cured nor diagnosed by the doctor; they go away on their own.

This environment — conditions of uncertainty and ambiguity, problems solving themselves as mysteriously as they arose — is not the exclusive province of medicine. Every parent, teacher, and administrator recognizes it. What is important about medicine is the willingness — nay, the necessity — of informing the decision-making process with facts and careful analysis insofar as it can, and only then relying on intuition. Because the education knowledge base has been so incomplete, teachers, administrators, and board members often are forced to fly by the seat of their pants. In a school lucky enough to hire or find people with finely honed intuition, the approach works well. But it is not a formula for a mass enterprise.

Peter Drucker observes that the task of education is to make ordinary people do extraordinary things. He is right. But to do this on a large scale requires systematic approaches to solving problems. That is why the idea of standards, choice, and technology converge in the overarching idea of "knowledge-based decision making." Decision makers must understand where the proper locus of decision making resides and where are the limits of knowledge, both derived from science and intuition.

The proper locus is captured in the awkward term *subsidiarity*. It means to make the decision as close to the problem (or opportunity) as possible. It means pushing decision making down the organizational hierarchy as close to the "work face" as possible. It means empowering teachers and building administrators. It means an end to micromanagement. It means freeing senior administrators and board members from day-to-day concerns and giving them responsibility for the big picture.

The "limits of knowledge" question is not so complex as it might at first appear. It is not a matter of perfect decision making scientifically arrived at; it is a matter of consistently good decision making over time. Indeed, as political scientists know, waiting for perfect decisions makes "the perfect the enemy of the good." The secret is to seek as good information as can be found, analyze it, and change or modify interventions as appropriate. For example, Title I programs do not have to be "pullout" programs; inventive and resourceful schools have begun to offer them as after-school programs. The idea makes pedagogical and social sense and is certainly worth trying. And it is worth studying as well.

In the final analysis, schools will never be run scientifically in the way a huge laboratory or nuclear submarine is. To the contrary, they should not be. Good schools will continue to be loosely connected institutions that rely on improvisation and professional judgments that are normative, not technical. But they should self-consciously and deliberately do what medicine has done — they should look for scientifically valid and replicable findings where they can be found and use them for making decisions where they can. At the same time, they should be forthcoming about the limits of science and own up to what is science and what is art. Clearly much of what goes on in a primary school is "art"; the warmth and affection of a good teacher is not scientifically derived. But there is much about the instructional program that can be illuminated by careful study. The current debates about phonics, bilingual education, OBE, and the like, could be sensibly advanced, even resolved, with carefully crafted research protocols.

A final cautionary note is order. A failure to organize and conduct careful research puts the whole enterprise at risk. Take Title I. It is hard to imagine a better-intentioned program. Math and reading services for the poor and dispossessed. Who needs them more? How could scarce public resources be better targeted? That, of course, is the question that educators and policy analysts must be able to answer. What kind of "bang for the buck" is there? Resources are finite, and it is reasonable to examine program impact. And the examinations of Title I that have been completed are not encouraging. More than $100 million and a third of a century old, Title I does not reveal any "sustaining effects." Why not? It may be an artifact of the program — it is so diverse in implementation that Title I exists only in statute and not in reality, a sort of Platonic ideal that has never come to earth. It may be that the research has been poorly designed and executed. Or, God forbid, it may be that the program has no intellectual starch and is all a big mistake.

The real mistake, of course, is to design and put in place a program based on a set of assumptions that do not pan out or cannot be measured. President Johnson thought, in good faith, that Title I would improve the lives of poor children. It may have, in ways that the research has not found. But to report, as the new century dawns, that the most ambitious federal government program in the history of elementary and secondary education has "no sustaining effects" invites cynicism and puts Title I itself at risk.

10

Choice in education would be simple were it not for the ideological baggage it carries. It would be about markets, willing consumers and willing buyers. In the economy at large and in the culture itself, choice involves two sets of actors: providers and clients. In education, choice is a transaction between students and schools. This thumbnail sketch describes higher education, not lower education. In the world of elementary and secondary education (unlike preschool and postsecondary education) the state is the principal supplier of education services. The reasons for this are old and deep, and space does not permit a careful review in this essay. Suffice it to say that in the arcane terms of political science, the argument is best framed in the classical language of liberty and equality. Those who incline toward liberty incline toward choice; those who emphasize equality prefer government schools.

But there is another element of choice that is important in the post-capitalist world (as Peter Drucker describes it). And that is choice as a kind of economic activity; and like all modern economic activity, technology is a central part of the process. Before turning to this theme, however, it is useful to strip choice of its ideological trappings and examine choice functionally.

In democracies, at least, choice is a key element in most transactions between providers and clients: Doctors are chosen by patients, universities by students, architects by clients, lawyers by plaintiffs, stores by customers, churches by congregants, and so on. There is no mystery as to why this is so: People prefer it. There is no mystery as to how it works: Willing providers and willing clients come together because each has something to gain from the other. The transaction is voluntary and, insofar as it is satisfactory, it continues.

Indeed, just as choice is the key to democracy, it lies at the very heart of markets. It has become fashionable in liberal circles to pooh-pooh markets, fashionable in conservative circles to exalt them. Because neither side has a monopoly on truth or virtue, it is useful to think about those aspects of markets that have a bearing on schooling. At their best, what do markets do? Regarding schools, there are five major dimensions to effective markets.

First and foremost, markets are exquisitely calibrated communication systems, letting willing buyers know what is available and willing sellers know what is wanted. They continuously transmit information about availability, cost, quality, and quantity. To be sure, markets are not perfect; but there are mechanisms to smooth over the rough spots. Word of mouth is powerful in its own right and can be supplemented by consumer guides and truth in advertising requirements. Products and services that do not perform as promised soon disappear from the market.

49

Second, in a functioning market, cost does not determine price, an idea foreign to most non-economists. This simple formulation, however, is what distinguishes a monopoly from a competitive market. The monopolist charges what he likes; and if consumers "need" the monopolist's product or service, the monopolist is in the catbird seat. By way of contrast, in functioning markets there are no despots who can pick the customer's pocket, no one who can force the customer to pay a price he thinks is too dear. The customer finds another provider, substitutes, or does without. The supplier, by way of contrast, must push his costs below the consumer's "price point" if he plans to stay in business. Although the consumer is king, in this formulation, "profit" is the entrepreneur's reward for getting the mix of product quality, availability, and price "right."

Third, niches, specialty places within the larger market, characterize functioning markets. Not just Tiffany or Cartier, but specialty providers of all kinds — farmer's markets on the weekend, Montessori schools in an otherwise uniform private school market, e-commerce firms such as Lands End, and so on. Participants in markets can realize economies of scale when production runs are long and demand is strong, but niches are equally important for they reflect special tastes and interests of both consumers and producers.

Fourth is Viennese economist Joseph Schumpeter's great insight. The single most important thing that markets provide is "creative destruction." Goods or services providers who do not satisfy their customers either change their ways or go out of business. No other form of social organization does this (at least in a peaceful fashion). To the contrary, when social decisions are made by political processes, the squeaky wheel gets the grease. Incompetence is as often rewarded as not. How else explain the existence of schools in our central cities that no one who had the means to leave would attend? Only a monopoly could keep such institutions open.

Fifth and most important is entrepreneurship, a coinage of French economist Georges Says. He needed a term to describe the innovator and inventor who brings new products or services to market that no one — till that time — knew they needed. In the modern era the Xerox machine, the fax machine, the World Wide Web, and the laptop computer are examples. Indeed, Chester Carlson, inventor of Xerography, had a difficult time finding investors because most people thought there was no market for plain paper copies. Notably, the entrepreneur swims upstream; he or she is going against the current. To be successful they need two key ingredients: a market that will not crush them in the development phase, and one that will reward them — by adopting and utilizing the fruits of entrepreneurship — when the product or service is ready. It hardly needs noting that government organizations are not favorably disposed toward internal entrepreneurship; they neither encourage it nor reward it.

Note my silence on matters of profit — nonprofit organizations are subject to market forces as well. A museum that displays great art is greeted by great demand. A museum with poor or bad taste will not keep its doors open long. So, too, with private schools. Truth be told,

51

the distinction in the world of education is not critical. They can go either way, profit or not-for-profit. There are more than 25,000 private schools in the nation and only a tiny handful — several hundred at most — are for-profit. This is not the place to examine all the reasons that contribute to this situation. In part it is an artifact of our tax laws, in part it is the heavy hand of custom. It is also the case that most Americans do not like to think of capitalists making a "profit" on their children. Suffice it to say that the vast, overwhelming majority of providers and clients prefer nonprofit to profit-making schools.

But if choice is intellectually interesting, it remains a political non-starter. In the modern era, it has been debated seriously since the release of Rose and Milton Friedman's path-breaking 1954 book, *Capitalism and Freedom*. To Chicago-school economists, the arguments the Friedmans marshal are compelling, yet the body politic has not been moved to support public school choice schemes except on the most modest scale. American culture, history, and legal traditions have exerted a powerful brake on school choice. It falls to technology, the concluding section of this essay, to change the debate.

11

Technology — it is important to establish at the outset — is a tool, a means to an end, not an end in itself. Its use must be guided by normative decisions that are based on thoughtful judgment. A pen is part of writing technology, no less than a word processor, yet human intervention is required. A pen does not move itself. As Robert Benchley wryly noted when asked, "Isn't it difficult to write?" "Why no, you simply write whatever occurs to you. It's the occurring that's hard."

The notion that technology is the handmaiden, not the master, while true is incomplete. It is also the case that such distinctions obscure as much as they reveal. Truth be told, transforming technologies quickly assume lives of their own, overwhelming and setting aside old ways of doing things. They bring about qualitative changes in both the way we do things and what we do.

For example, until the invention of the steam engine, commerce and communications moved at the speed a horse could walk (or, for short distances, trot). Steam power made it possible to move large cargoes across land (and larger cargoes at sea); it set the stage for corresponding developments — the telegraph (which brought an end to the Pony Express, a quixotic enterprise in which horses carried feather-weight messages at great speed. The adventure, a part of American folklore to this day, lasted a scant 18 months).

The modern era — and the coming era, as far as we can see — is characterized by transforming technologies in the worlds of entertainment, health care, commerce, transportation, and communication. Technology is only beginning to make itself felt in the world of education. Higher education provides a glimpse of the future of elementary and secondary education. Already "electronic content delivery" is taken for granted. Rare is the college or university that does not offer at least some coursework online. Rarer yet is the higher education institution that does not use high technology to manage its affairs. And use of the Internet and access to laptop computers is now taken for granted in many colleges and universities because it is required. Incoming freshmen must bring a laptop with them — or, as is commonly done now — they will be issued a laptop when they arrive. They are expected to be in regular touch with their professors, each other, and the Internet from the day they arrive.

Modern computing and telecommunications capabilities make it possible to manage large, complex data sets "on time and online," which themselves influence the nature of decision making. There is a powerful reciprocal at work. Computers, modems, servers, and the right software make it possible to know what is going on anywhere, anytime in any school (and any school district) in the local system, the state, or the nation.

If technology is not an end in itself, it is a tool of such power that it transforms all that it touches. It provides intellectual leverage — if that is what it is used for. But it is noteworthy that in the world of elementary and secondary education, technology is most conspicuous by its absence (perhaps like the Sherlock Holmes dog that didn't bark). Technology in most schools is weakly conceived and poorly executed. At issue is not just management technology — that, too, is only unevenly used — but instructional technology for content delivery. That is the unfulfilled promise of the IT (information technology) revolution. To date, technology-based content for children is almost exclusively found in electronic games, both at home and in video arcades. The technology that makes them possible can deliver instruction as readily as it does games, but it has not been used because the culture of schooling neither invites nor welcomes it. But that is changing. Witness the most significant policy decision to affect schools in the past one-third of a century — since Lyndon Johnson's Great Society ushered in a major federal role.

It has been little noted and little remarked upon. E-rate, a six-billion-dollar investment in its first three years, has no end in sight. It was not avidly sought after before its enactment in 1997, nor was its effect fully anticipated. But it has already lead to wholesale changes in schooling and public policy toward school. E-rate monies are made available to schools, public and private, for Internet connectivity and hard wiring for LANS (local area networks). The funds are derived from a telecommunications surcharge that appears on everyone's long distance phone bill. Technically not a tax, it is collected by the FCC and rebated on a formula basis. The funds are made available on a sliding scale, with poor schools receiving more than prosperous schools. (The only outright disqualification is schools with endowments in excess of $50 million.) Private schools are permitted to receive funds as public schools do because the funds are not from tax sources. As a consequence, no church-state separation issue arises. The whole process is presumptively constitutional.

From a wholly unexpected source, then, comes a technology "fix" that is genuinely transformative. Not just as a technology, but in its policy implications. E-rate blurs — nay, obliterates — the historic distinction between public and private schools, and home schooling cannot be far behind. And additional technology policies are likely to do more of the same, at both the state and federal levels. The E-rate authorization has two more years to run, and the likelihood of a reauthorization is high. What might the contours of reauthorization look like? In part, more of the same. That, of course, is vintage Washington. But there is likely to be something new as well. The technology issue on everyone's lips today is the digital divide. Like Potter Stewart's famous dictum about pornography — it is hard to define, but you know it when you see it — the digital divide is hard to define. In its most generous meaning the term is meant to describe haves and have-nots in the technology world — poor children (and poor teachers, for that matter) who do not have access to high-powered computers and the Internet.

The most obvious "fix" is to give poor students and teachers free or reduced-price computers and Internet access from home. The instrumentalities to accomplish this are many, in both the public and private sector. Indeed, in April of 2000 President Clinton announced a $100 million program of private sector gifts of computers and software to do exactly that. Kicked off by Hewlett Packard with a promise of $15 million over the first three years, other high-tech firms are stepping up to the plate.

The obvious role for Uncle Sam is to continue to subsidize Internet use, not just from school but from home as well. The technology exists to subsidize dial-up protocols, either through 800 numbers or through a local school number. Students (and their families) would not need their own ISP (Internet Server Provider) account.

The technology for cheap Internet use is readily available, even if it is not yet rolling off the assembly line. As cheap as laptops and PCs have become, there is more inexpensive technology yet: "dumb" terminals. A keyboard and modem connection (with a screen connection as well) can do the job. No computer is necessary — the central server, accessed over the ISP — can hold application files as well as an active "digital locker" for the user. Laptop loaners may also be used, but the dumb terminal and digital locker permit low-cost "thin" access on an unprecedented scale.

IT on this scale — everyone with access, seven days a week, 24 hours a day, from home, school, or on the road — represents a breakthrough with extraordinary potential. Content will be important, instantaneous communication will be important, but most important will be the fact that IT renders schools *transparent*. This term of computer art describes two phenomena simultaneously. A computer transaction is transparent in the sense that what produces the image on the screen is not visible to the user — in other words, users don't need to be expert in computer technology to use one. Laypersons can use them readily and comfortably, just as a person need not be expert in telephony to use a telephone.

The other meaning of transparent is even more important — properly trained, with the right hardware and software configuration, a user can use a computer to see "inside" an organization. For example, with the right software and modest training a school board member (or a journalist, for that matter) can identify test score results by age, race, school, free-lunch status, over time, or all of the above. That is, whatever is available on the computer can be presented, almost instantaneously, in a relational database that provides hitherto inaccessible information.

This is the kind of computational and analytic power the private sector (and much of government, excepting only schools) takes for granted. Just as a brokerage house can analyze millions of transactions a second or a mail order house can processes countless orders (and manage inventory at the same time), schools can begin to use information technology as an administrative and instructional resource without peer.

Transparency means that policy makers and practitioners can know both what is going on and what the effect of policy and practice is. Transparency completes the circle of performance-driven institutions. As I have suggested, a new triptych describes performance-driven schools. If standards, assessments, and consequences are the defining characteristics of performance-driven schools, modern relational databases and powerful computing makes rational decision making possible. No longer will educators have to wait six months for stale test scores to reach their desks as they do in many districts today.

The only thing that stands in the way of realizing these examples is the heavy hand of current practice. Unless schools are held accountable, the incentive to generate, store, and use data strategically is slight. With accountability the incentives increase. But the most powerful incentives to use data wisely and well must be generated internally. Educators must be convinced that data is useful, even valuable.

The question in the forefront of taxpayer and legislators' minds is, What are we getting for what we are spending? In most jurisdictions the honest answer is that nobody knows. The promise of the telecommunications revolution is that soon everyone will (or can) know.

The telecommunications revolution, then, will sweep aside the tired debates of the last century. It will give substance to standards, it will lay the foundations for knowledge-based decision making, and it will eliminate the choice debate as we know it. True, vouchers and choice will not disappear as issues, but they will be rationalized. Access to the full range of IT — for example, unlimited Internet access from home as well as from school — is the ultimate voucher.

12

It would be easy to predict a bleak future for American public education. Extrapolation from current trends is not encouraging. But simple extrapolation is almost always wrong. I am convinced that what we are seeing now is the storm before the lull. American education is troubled today precisely because it has done so well before; as a consequence, we expect much of it. Not long ago, the most highly educated person in the community was the teacher, and on him or her we lavished respect and deference. In community after community today, the teacher is only one of many highly educated people. That this is so is a commentary on how well the schools have done (and on how highly prized education is in the modern economy).

We are participating in a process of dramatic change, from an input-driven system to an output-driven system. And change is hard. Big change is harder yet. Truth be told, even those who give lip service to the wonders of "change" prefer "having changed" to "changing." So it comes as no surprise that we live in difficult times. But the promise is great. The benefits of an output-driven system are manifold, for teachers, students, and the larger society.

This essay has examined several themes, some ordinary, one elevated. The ordinary themes are standards, knowledge-based decision making, choice, and technology.

The "elevated" theme is the curriculum of the future: American elementary and secondary schools must reclaim their legacy. They must be liberal arts institutions in which students learn a few things very well: to read, to write, to listen, to speak, to manipulate symbols (mathematical and scientific), to master a second language, and to enter the world of art and music with confidence and pleasure. They must lay the foundations of wisdom by imparting knowledge. Knowledge is more than facts and figures; it is the capacity to understand what you have learned, including knowing how little you know. There is no such thing as understanding, or higher-order thinking, or problem solving without the fundamental knowledge of facts and their relationships. Problem solving, careful analysis, constructive communication, creativity, innovation, synthesis, thoughtful criticism does not exist *in vacuo*. To suppose they do would be like supposing that we could think without language.

Permit me to conclude with an Arabic apothegm:

He who knows not, and knows not that he knows not, is a fool. Shun him.

He who knows not, and knows that he knows not, is simple. Teach him.

He who knows, and knows not that he knows, is asleep. Waken him.

He who knows, and knows that he knows, is wise. Follow him.

To become liberally educated, students must know and master the great documents of citizenship from Plato's *Republic* to the *Magna Carta* to Lincoln's *Second Inaugural* to Martin Luther King's *Letter from Birmingham Jail*. They also must study the great documents of prose and poetry of East and West, just as they must master algebra, geometry, statistics, and probability. They must understand the scientific method, basic philosophy, and American and world history in scope and sequence. Most important, they must *know and understand*. Knowing and understanding is the basis of our moral compass; and it is the moral compass that distinguishes us from the rest of nature. Indeed, that is what education is all about.

There is a body of knowledge and understanding — and deeply held democratic values — that all American high school graduates must possess to be successful workers, good citizens, and productive members of their communities.

In the global economy of the next century they need no less. They deserve no less. Whether they receive no less depends on society at large. If the body politic is committed to high-quality schools, we will have them. If not, we will not. In a democracy, the schools we want are the schools we get. And the schools we get are the schools we deserve.

Recent Books Published by the
Phi Delta Kappa Educational Foundation

Vouchers, Class Size Reduction, and Student Achievement
Alex Molnar
Trade paperback. $12 (PDK members, $9)

Torsten Husén: Conversations in Comparative Education
Arild Tjeldvoll
Cloth with dust jacket. $49 (PDK members, $38)
Trade paperback. $24 (PDK members, $18)

French Elementary Education and the Ecole Moderne
William B. Lee and John Sivell
Trade paperback. $12 (PDK members, $9)

Readings on Leadership in Education
From the Archives of Phi Delta Kappa International
Trade paperback. $22 (PDK members, $16.50)

Profiles of Leadership in Education
Mark F. Goldberg
Trade paperback. $22 (PDK members, $16.50)

**Use Order Form on Next Page
Or Phone 1-800-766-1156**

*A processing charge is added to all orders.
Prices are subject to change without notice.*

Complete online catalog at http://www.pdkintl.org

Order Form

<table>
<tr><td colspan="4">SHIP TO:</td></tr>
<tr><td colspan="4">STREET</td></tr>
<tr><td colspan="4">CITY/STATE OR PROVINCE/ZIP OR POSTAL CODE</td></tr>
<tr><td colspan="3">DAYTIME PHONE NUMBER</td><td>PDK MEMBER ROLL NUMBER</td></tr>
</table>

QUANTITY	TITLE		PRICE

ORDERS MUST INCLUDE PROCESSING CHARGE	SUBTOTAL
Total Merchandise — *Processing Charge* $3 to $25 — $3 $25.01 to $100 — $5 Over $100 — 5% of total	Indiana residents add 5% Sales Tax
Special shipping available upon request. Prices subject to change without notice.	PROCESSING CHARGE
	TOTAL

☐ Payment Enclosed (check payable to Phi Delta Kappa International)

Bill my ☐ VISA ☐ MasterCard ☐ American Express ☐ Discover

ACCT #   DATE

		/				

EXP DATE   SIGNATURE

Mail or fax your order to: Phi Delta Kappa International,
P.O. Box 789, Bloomington, IN 47402-0789. USA
Fax: (812) 339-0018. Phone: (812) 339-1156

For fastest service, phone 1-800-766-1156 and use your credit card.